IN MIDNIGHT'S STILLNESS

VERSES WOVEN WITH LOVE, INTROSPECTION, AND THE UNFILTERED DEPTHS OF EMOTION

PRAKHAR TRIPATHI

To my parents, friends and family.

Thank you for always having my back.

Contents

Preface

From the very start, I have been quite an introvert (well, it feels strange—but somehow relieving—to admit this, perhaps for the first time). I kept to myself, never taking much interest in what others were doing. Many mistook this for self-centeredness. A school teacher once told me I was too absorbed in myself. It shouldn't have bothered me, but somehow, those words have lingered with me till now.

Amidst these perceptions of me, I found refuge in words—where I could be vulnerable without judgment. I remember the story behind my first poem, the first set of words that somehow came together meaningfully and unlocked my understanding and way of expression on a level I had never imagined. It was late in the evening, I was sitting restlessly on my chair, waiting—watching the hours slip by, unable to shake the restlessness creeping in. But if that restlessness hadn't been there, would I have found poetry? I seriously doubt it. I tried to focus on something else, anything else, but the lingering thoughts refused to fade. And then, all of a sudden, a few words unveiled themselves before me, as if they had been waiting to be found.

"I waited for the message,
I waited for the reply,
she asked me to be less expecting,
So became I."

And then there was an unusual comfort in my heart. I completed the poem, my first, which I have included in the chapter, *"Reflections & Confessions"*, something which I can never forget. I was sixteen back then.

I continued writing, and even shared a few of them with my teachers, when I got a comment I remember till date. He was my English teacher, Mr. Tribhuvan Mendiratta. He said, *"If pen flows continuously and so do the emotions, you'll yourself realize a new Prakhar within you."* I might not have understood what he meant that day, and maybe I never will—not fully. But if writing has taught me anything, it's that some answers are not meant to be found, only felt. Perhaps the 'new Prakhar' isn't someone I'll wake up and recognize one day, but someone I'm constantly becoming, one poem at a time.

I have always believed in signs. Perhaps that's why I feel drawn to the night sky—for even in the coldest of nights, looking up feels like a warm embrace, a quiet reassurance that I am safe. Many of the pieces in this book emerged from these moments—roaming in the dark, under the watchful eyes of the stars, lost in thought, trying to untangle the threads of my mind and make sense of them.

This collection is not just a set of poems—it is a journey through love, solitude, fear, and hope. Each piece carries fragments of my thoughts, confessions left unsaid, and reflections I've found in the silence of my mind. There is a certain comfort in the vastness of the universe, in knowing that we are all fleeting beings in infinity. Yet, within that vastness, our emotions—love, longing, memories—feel infinite in their own unique way. This book is my attempt to capture that paradox, to embrace both the immensity of existence and the quiet whispers of the heart.

These poems were written over four years. Some may seem naïve, some a little more refined. But I have chosen to keep them all, as they are—honest, raw, and reflective of the person I was and the person I am becoming. Forgive me, perhaps, for keeping them all.

Some of these poems may speak to you, some may echo feelings you once had, and some may leave you with questions—just as they did for me. Whatever you take from these pages, I hope you find a piece of yourself in them, just as I have found pieces of myself in writing them.

"These words are echoes of unspoken moments, confined within the cage of my heart, at last finding their way out.
Treat them gently, as if they were whispers intended only for you."

Acknowledgements

I am deeply grateful to those who have been part of this journey—through its highs and lows. Some have been with me from the very beginning, while others joined along the way, encouraging me to believe in my words and my capabilities.

To my parents, **Mr. Sanjeev Kumar Tripathi** and **Mrs. Mamta Tripathi**, your unwavering support has been my foundation, always nurturing my passion. To my siblings, my constant source of strength—thank you for being my safe space.

A heartfelt thank you to my teachers, who instilled in me the confidence to believe, *yes, I can do this*.

And to my friends—you have uplifted me, inspired me, and reminded me why I write. In many ways, this book belongs to you as much as it does to me. Thank you for being my people.

1. Reflections and Confessions

"A journey within, where thoughts echo, confessions remain unheard, and reflections shape the soul."

So Became I

I waited for the message,
I waited for the reply,
she asked me to be less expecting,
So became I.
Trying to overcome, trying to breathify,
to be accepted by this world,
So became I.
All frustrated, I questioned why,
for the sake of someone else,
to be embraced by this world,
Did I become I.

Ambiguity

It was early morning,

as I was wide awake,

The birds appeared to have started their chores,

for it couldn't be more peaceful without a mistake.

I looked up above,

a sense of clarity it bestowed,

something which I lack in abundance lately,

as I absentmindedly strolled.

History did repeat itself,

just feeding the fear inside me,

and I did nothing but smile,

for it easily hides the pain, you see.

The fear isn't about acceptance,

It's more of a personal scrutiny,

it's not about that "someone",

for it's me who's left with nothing but ambiguity.

I am scared,

of connecting with people emotionally,

with people who are bound to leave,

for you always get a feeling eventually.

And sometimes,

All of a sudden, they're back,

Back with those loads of memories,

which once you wished to forget, without a track.
Meanwhile, the sun has shown its presence,
the sky brightly lit,
There're still some clouds up there,
The resemblance brings a smile, if only a bit.

You

Standing by the door,
with your memories flooding my mind,
the rain chanting the tale,
When towards you, I inclined.
You are the reason for my happiness,
the reason behind my smile,
but that you'd become a habit—
I can't deny, not even in exile.
From strangers lost in the crowd
to sharing our untold story,
I never came this far with anyone,
but with you, I could walk even to a cemetery.
From celebrating my victories
to catching me when I was wrong,
even when anger clouded your face,
you never left me alone for long.
No, today is nothing special,
but I thought you should know—
even if our words grow fewer,
I'm always here, should you ever feel low.

How did We Grow Apart?

I was sitting in my room,
while I stared at the wall,
thinking how drastically my life had changed,
but without you, it feels like I'm about to fall.
For the first time, I had found someone,
with whom I felt so close with,
felt as if I had found a friend for life,
But hardly did I know, it was all a myth.
We used to share everything,
often lost count of time,
Now you're just going down the list,
Honestly speaking, it hurts a lot sometimes.
We promised to grow up together,
how did we grow apart then?
With you I felt a little less alone,
But now that feeling is magnified to ten.
I'm still trying to cope up,
For it feels I've lost a part of me,
No matter how my day was,
It feels a bit empty, you see.
But I'm grateful for the time I spent with you,
the times I had never even imagined,
because as they say,

"Don't be sad because it's over,
Smile because it happened."

Once, I Would Have Reached

She seemed sad,

But I didn't ask her why,

Maybe I knew she expected me to ask,

Did I let her down on purpose?

Proving her wrong,

when, despite anyone or anything,

I would have been the first to beseech,

Find ways to comfort her,

Or anyone, saying,

"You seem sad, let's go for a walk,

maybe talking it out saves you from the havoc",

When did I stop being me?

My heart frozen to an extent,

ending up finding comfort in its solace,

when it could've shown an intent.

Weight of unspoken words,

press against my chest,

a hidden fear surfaces itself,

whispering, "It will end just like the rest."

The Coffee Shop

The sun was up,

but the clouds covered it partially,

with frequent soft breaths of wind,

the weather was just in harmony.

I found a corner in the coffee shop,

after ordering my regular one,

took out my diary and a pen,

the best time of my day, and it had just begun.

I looked around,

and found peace in the chaos,

The setting seemed to have a magical effect,

And that coffee sip, as if saying the play's still on.

It's my go-to place, well, always has been,

but lately has become an escape,

with sudden urges to disconnect,

to know what's happening inside, to keep my mind in shape.

I wrote for a while,

to clear things off my head,

well, it did work to some extent,

felt as if I had already won the day ahead.

I got up,

my coffee was over a long time ago,

a cool breeze welcomed me,

as it cleared the remaining in its flow.

The Lighthouse You Are

The skepticism was at an all-time high,

had to be, I sighed,

A voice within trembled low,

nagging me, saying, "What if they don't know?",

knavish felt my words, incapable to show.

You comforted me gently,

often coming to the rescue,

understanding me when the world fails,

steady and kind, when none had a cue.

A pounding anxious heart found a home,

inside was peace it had never known,

yearning for understanding, at last, set free-

of late, emotions had ceased in me.

Garrulously I poured my heart your way,

in you, I found a place to stay,

through silence and storms, you remained,

A lighthouse in my stormy sea, guiding me home again.

2. Love and Longing

"Love, in its rawest form, is longing— an ache that resides in the heart, a comfort that feels like home."

And There She Was

And there she was,

an epitome of elegance,

like peace in the chaos,

like hope for the despondent,

emanating a ray of light,

warm enough to make you smile.

Her eyes deeper than the ocean,

carrying endless tales to be told,

her smile melting the coldest of hearts,

her presence pacified my soul,

her absence dimmed the same.

And there she was,

doing nothing,

still making my heart pound like anything,

so far away,

yet felt like a part of me.

And there she was,

effortlessly,

making me fall in love with her.

In the Wake of You

The splash of waves across the shore,

the sound,

the resonance,

the quietness that follows--

filling the empty void,

slowly with serenity,

taking everything in its wake.

My emotions peaked,

my eyelids rose,

were you real?

or a figment of imagination I suppose.

Mouth dry, feet frozen still,

hands trembling, beyond my will.

My eyes fixed only on you,

brown eyes, cosmic depth,

heavenly smile,

never seen such a beauty, I bet.

You came towards me,

striding softly,

stopping within an arm's length,

my heart at its best,

adding to the uneasiness,

Could she hear it beating?

Oh, what a mess!
The Gods must be eyeing this,
for she gave me a hug,
her embrace, as pure as a dove,
I felt something stir deep within,
a warmth unspoken, yet understood,
Is this what they call love?

The Paradoxical Warmth of Your Hand

The place was bustling,

with souls rummaging through one another,

the ones who always wanted to slow down,

Oh! The paradoxical mortals in their slumber.

You quickly held my hand,

your fingers intertwined with mine,

my eyes searched the sky to see,

Had the stars finally aligned?

You shortened the gap between us,

a rather big one in my mind,

but who cares about reality,

when your vision portrays,

when your mind is in denial,

the world around fades,

into oblivion of nothingness,

when right and wrong blur into nonexistence,

when all you desired was that warmth,

tending to you in its softness,

when it's the heart that speaks, filling in for the mouth,

for I clasped your hands tighter,

the nerves on your forehead relaxed,

a tear tracing its descent,

caught midair by the wind, it gasped.

The crowd cleared the way,
so did the mess within my mind,
but all of a sudden they came,
knocking me down,
for her hands, no longer in mine,
as I fell short of words to whine.

Just You

These dark evenings,
Cloudy skies,
With a blow on my face,
How I wish you were around my eyes.
No worries, no sorrows,
Just you in my arms,
Unescorted by the tensions of tomorrow.
This beautiful weather,
With lush greenery all around,
Did I spot a treasure??
When you, I found.
In a world where one betrays the other,
You came to me as if we were made for each other,
With you in my arms,
I feel like a needy getting his alms.
Thank you for everything you've done,
Thank you for making me a human,
Without you in my life,
I feel that I'm barely alive...

When my Heart broke for the first time

The night it dawned upon me,

the pen started to flow automatically,

my emotions came on the paper,

when the winds blew dramatically.

I thought you would come,

I thought you would show some,

but all you did was,

to tell me that you're done.

Something broke that day,

maybe never to heal again,

because someone with whom I dreamt everything,

told me that we need to separate our way.

I remember the day we met,

Oh my god!! How could I ever forget,

My eyes were stuck only upon you,

but never dared to say, "I love you".

But for me, you'll remain my soul always,

no matter what you show,

Because I know it's your anger that says.

Never had I dreamt that I would say,

"Sorry for everything I did,

and thank you for everything you did",

I gaze at the stars and wonder,

"When my love did a blunder".

3. Dreams and What-Ifs

"A world of imagined love, fleeting possibilities and unspoken desires where strangers feel familiar; a space for longing, hope, and the bittersweet magic of what if..."

Hope or Illusion?

He was standing by the side,

witnessing a mesmerizing sunset,

when suddenly a thought struck his head,

which made him quite upset.

He used to see her everywhere,

Be it a coffee shop or a restaurant,

Even while walking down an empty lane,

There wasn't a place for him, where she wasn't there.

He used to talk to her in his mind,

telling her about everything that happened,

He thought of being with her,

with her head on his shoulder, as he imagined.

But, was she a figment of his imagination,

Or does such perfection exist?

For it has become so much difficult for him lately,

to find a way for his mind and heart to coexist.

He still believes there is someone out there,

who would be as loving as him,

But isn't the hope he's holding onto almost impossible,

and above all of that, is he even aware?

Someday, Somewhere

It was a normal evening, I remember,

as I was watching the sunset,

the sky was entirely red,

And so were my cheeks, although I was a bit upset.

I was thinking, again,

of someone whom I always wanted to be mine,

That person isn't real, you know,

But my feelings are pure, no less than a shrine.

Maybe we would meet,

Like bumping into each other,

We won't be knowing anything about us,

Just a short sweet smile, but please do wait for me to recover.

Won't it be so honest,

Just two strangers conversing,

Might be about some of our long hidden secrets,

But no matter what, it would never have felt tiring.

We would be enjoying each other's company,

If possible, your hand held in mine,

I would be looking only at you,

Your eyes, hair, smile, wouldn't it be so divine.

I'm not sure if you would ever be mine,

Or if we would ever meet,

But ever if we collide,

I'm gonna show you this, for then only would this be complete.

A Fleeting Encounter

I was on my way on the train,

my mind weaving its own story,

It feels as if it's continuously on the run,

Or maybe there's something stormy.

There was a girl,

Sitting diagonally opposite to me,

Looking a bit lost in herself,

while her eyes nearly as deep as the sea.

She was beautiful, no doubt,

But not in the ordinary sense,

For her beauty was unparalleled,

I guess, I ought to add, no offense.

She was quiet all the way,

Mostly keeping to herself,

Yet she was intriguing,

creating sort of her realm.

Sadly, it's time to bid adieu,

As the train screeches to a halt,

It was a short sweet journey, I would say,

Quite contrary to what I thought.

For a Coffee, Maybe?

"It's been a long time", my pen whined,

"Why not write the truth you hide?",

at least there won't be any regret,

For she looks so beautiful in her attire,

Ohh!! You don't need any hints, why do I always forget?".

My eyes caught you sitting in a corner,

keeping to yourself much,

But when I saw your smile,

my adrenaline streamed like a gush.

You have a world of friends,

I have a few, maybe just one.

You're known wherever you go,

I stay in shadows, lost in none.

But there's something I've always wished for,

and today, I ask—

Can I take you out somewhere?

I promise, it won't be far,

maybe just for a coffee,

and then I'll walk you home.

I know I'm not perfect,

but does that word even mean anything?

I'll try my best to make you laugh,

because your smile—

that's what matters most.

And it's okay if you don't want to—
no pressure, no expectations.
But maybe someday,
you'll say yes,
and we'll sit across each other,
with coffee between us,
and time standing still.

Best Day

I could hear it beating,

felt as if, any moment it would pop out,

because that day had finally come,

for which my heart has done nothing but shout.

Of all the alternatives I had,

black was destined to win,

for I had to give my best look,

After all, I was taking you out, a long struggle it's been.

I took my seat in the coffee shop,

Trying to calm myself down,

Though I love to talk, but

When it comes to girls, my record isn't that profound.

I was just pulling up my sleeves,

When you entered,

"How could someone look so beautiful?",

was the question with which my brain was centered.

We exchanged smiles,

While we sat down facing each other,

It was the time our eyes met,

provoking the only thought then, "How could I not love her?".

From talking about the best moments we had,

To eventually creating one,

Though our mugs were already empty a long time ago,

But it was noticed by none.

All I wanted was to look at you,

Your face, your eyes, your smile,

I could adore it all day,

How I wished the time would have stopped, only for a while.

We got up, as we were about to leave,

For our eyes met once again,

But my heart nearly did melt down,

When you came forward and hugged me tight then.

It was the best day I ever had,

With happiness pouring down as rain,

But I had to bring it to a pause soon, you know,

Ohh!! Didn't I mention that I was dreaming again?

Still Holding On

The wind blew swiftly today,

No it wasn't a cool breeze,

Neither was it raining, I remember,

But felt as if my heart was about to freeze.

I have stopped reacting lately,

to whatever is going around,

It appears as if there's a loop,

with me constantly running,

But trust me, it isn't that profound.

Yesss it's true that I loved her,

But it never felt the same from her,

No, I wasn't ignored as well,

But, she never accepted me, as if she didn't care.

Yaa!! I know all this happens,

"You can't force anyone to love you",

But sometimes, it hurts like hell, you know,

When you wanna tell something, but to whom?

I don't know if she's still there or not,

but now it feels a bit odd,

Maybe I'm the one who's overthinking,

How I thought that anything could break but not that bond.

Still, whenever I think of her,

That same old smile comes to my face,

When I used to look at her,
And did nothing but embrace.

4. Shadows of the Mind

"These poems are echoes of fears we suppress, thoughts we bury, moments when the world feels distant, and we find ourselves searching for meaning in the solitude."

Alone

Even in the midst of everyone,

It feels that there is no one.

Nobody to share our feelings with,

Nobody to convey our thoughts,

Nobody to hear our musings,

Nobody to understand that we are overwrought.

Alone,

Alone in this world of irony,

Just me and my shadow,

Giving each other a company,

It's high time to understand,

That it's only you who can love you without a demand,

After all,

Even amidst crowd of all-mine,

There is none to confide time.

The Time When the Head met the Pillow

The head went down
full of stress,
Every part of the body ached,
As if it were made to compress.

The pillow, seeing him sympathetically, said,
"Oh, baby! Come on, I'll cure all your distress.
The head trusted the pillow,
thought, "He must be right", and so was his guess.

The moment he touched the pillow,
Wondered, was it a bless,
for all his anxieties,
for all his uneasiness,
just got undressed.

The head got emotional and started crying,
but again came the pillow at rescue,
Absorbing every tear overlying.
The pillow consoled the head and said,
"In this world of obscurities,
Brave is one who fights,
Fights, no matter ahead be all the severities."

Meanwhile the body relished the show,
The time when the head met the pillow.

Night Time

"The clock struck twelve,
a sense of stillness outside,
with winds gushing past the trees,
a new world I enter" - he sighed.

"This world is mine,
where I feel the most alone,
I don't know how to overcome it,
But it's where overthinking's a cyclone."

"Earlier I was able to sleep peacefully,
But what happened to me suddenly,
The boy who used to ignore the rubbish,
Now feels there's nothing to relish."

The boy started sobbing,
while saying this to himself,
felt he had no one,
Who could love him without being selfish.

His mother was listening at the door,
She came closer and hugged him tight,
and said, "Don't you worry any more,
For I'll always be there in your every fight."

He placed his head over her lap,
with she patting him lovingly,
He dozed off for a long nap,
like a warrior returning victoriously.

We Are All Just Running

We are all just running,

some away from their homes,

maybe cause they feel suffocated there,

while some towards one,

as a shelter, for if they run away from somewhere.

We are all just running,

some away from responsibilities,

for they find them a burden,

while some towards them,

since they are who people look up to, like a devotee listening

to a sermon.

We are all just running,

some from their lovers,

for their worth wasn't realised,

while some in search of them,

for all they want is to be accepted without being rationalized.

We are all just running,

some from reality,

finding solace in their little world,

while some out of time,

struggling for their breath, as their vision gets blurred.

We are all just running,

some after success,

for they fear facing failure,

and some from life,

just as in front of a violent sea is a helpless sailor.

Trapped in a Whirlpool of Thoughts

I feel so tired,

contemplating the mess within,

will I ever be able to get out of this whirlpool,

sometimes all I can think is, when?

A series of chores left halfway,

kinda troubles me,

the task of carrying everyone and everything,

oh! Is there anywhere else I could be?

On this, a friend once asked me,

"Are you scared of commitment?

For you tend to run from things,

when they show a chance of fulfilment."

So, I became distant,

blindly adding yet another thing to my bag,

being tired of rethinking all the mess within,

stuck in a whirlpool of unending thoughts,

Oh! Will I ever be able to get out or should I say, in?

Shattered

The glass dangled in my fingers,
safeguarding what lay within,
but how long can it uphold itself,
aphonic is its struggle,
beleaguered, unescaped.
The fingers it once deemed a blessing,
ephemeral it was,
quietly tightening their grip,
eyeing their way inside.
The glass could no longer bear it.
Its content now amorphous,
leaving the fingers red.
Its final, fatal attempt,
Oh! What havoc trust begets.

The Weight of Silence

The silence is alluring,

quite peculiar it is,

pulling me closer,

rekindling something lost within.

A double-edged sword,

wounding as it heals,

for did I find myself?

away from mortals haunting,

embedding their claws,

or did I lose myself?

plummeting into darkness,

the old me, convivial,

erased from existence,

a bleak memory of the past.

I sit here,

circumambient by my thoughts,

my constant companion,

for are they a friend or foe?

dragging me into negligence,

away from beings,

I call my own.

I feel stifled,

the emptiness a bit agonizing.

Have I sinned,
Too grave to be forgiven?
Or is it the start of something,
where I end up riven?

5. Echoes of the Past

"Memories linger like whispers in the wind—some warm, some haunting."

This chapter captures moments that time cannot erase, reflections of what once was and what remains within us.

Memories

You were standing at the bus stop,

with me just staring at you,

Though the world was moving on,

but my heart was glued only upon you.

Your eyes still had the same sparkle,

which once mesmerized me,

How can I ever forget that eye contact,

My whole life changed, you know Baby.

The first time I held your hand in mine,

I had a feeling,

I couldn't express that in words,

But I'm sure that my heart was healing.

You promised you would stay,

looking straight into my eyes,

but hardly was I knowing,

that all of a sudden,

You'll go away.

A child came running towards her,

and she hugged him, steadied,

He has got the same eyes as hers,

Ohh!! Didn't I mention that she is married?

Brown Eyes

I saw her today,

quietly standing at the bus stop,

her body being at peace with the surroundings,

while her eyes,

her brown eyes seemed breathtaking,

as the light fell onto that heavenly piece.

She knew I was an overthinker,

doubted myself more than anybody else,

yet, she never cared to ask,

"How have you been doing lately, mister?",

something she always failed to express.

I wanted to ask her,

"Don't you ever think of me?",

might wanna check up on,

as for me,

I'm a mess,

like an unstable Jenga tower, just about to crumble,

my brain's clogged with things,

I'm not convinced I deserve,

all good and bad included, as I recall.

I don't tell people things,

slowly engulfing my inside,

for I fear,

they might use it to hurt me,

well, hasn't it always been the case, my heart replied.

So all I do is smile,

as I watched you board the bus,

knowing that your brown eyes did notice me,

long before I did,

as I smiled at my existence turning into dust.

And There I Stood

And there I stood,

looking at her,

standing close to him,

displaying a rather short, shy smile,

when it should've been me,

tenderly holding her in my arms,

a ship resting peacefully in its harbour;

when it should've been me,

gently caressing her hair,

only to get a feel of her face;

when it should've been me,

looking in her eyes,

finding myself lost in the eternal depths of her serenity.

They say,

maybe she was the right person at the wrong time,

but wasn't everything supposed to be right then?

So I smiled,

looking at her being calm and happy,

oblivious to the fact,

that there did create a void in me, never to be filled again,

as I stood there intact.

Fading into Yesterday

I felt a bit alienated,

as if I shouldn't have been here,

The world I called so dearly mine,

appeared foggy, more than my eyes could bear.

They had learnt to live without me,

their world undecipherable,

For I was a mere character,

when once I too had been with them, inseparable.

Did I crave to be heard?

Did I yearn to be chosen?

Why am I the way I am?

Ending up like this, turning around to find no one.

I remember the laughs we had,

the moments we have carved in our hearts,

Now, lost in the echoes of yesterday,

perhaps it's the passage of time,

which does this in parts.

I sit quietly,

a mute spectator to this,

with voices screaming inside me,

to stay,

promising I'll be better,

to not leave me in this abyss.

The Amorist's Lament

I zoomed in on you,

Your smile radiating peace in the polaroid,

What would that look like now?

which once provided warmth to my cold heart,

which once gave shelter to my peregrine soul,

lighting the dark aisles of my memories,

making my dead eyes roll.

How would that feel now?

which once solaced my heart,

a sense of familiarity to one who's lost,

an enchanting spell,

the crowded alleys devoid of thoughts.

What would its absence feel like?

The weight of unspoken words,

bends her mouth,

but the eyes whisper tales,

only the lost can listen aloud.

I am an amorist,

beshrewed by fate,

as I glanced at you,

that smile- too distant to cherish, too familiar to hate.

And In That Moment

And in that moment,
I knew,
I was over her,
for her eyes no longer had that charm,
her hair possessed an ordinary odour,
for her hands seemed normal,
which once had dazzled me,
just like the weather in October.
And in that moment,
I smiled,
probably after a very long time,
for that smile contained acceptance,
and a bit of dejection too,
for she was no longer mine,
or was she ever?
Well! That's a nice view.

Lingering Echoes

I stepped into the room,

my footsteps echoed a hollow sigh,

walls closing in on every side,

not a soul nearby.

Then, out of nowhere, they appeared,

huddled around the table,

laughter spilling between them,

lost in a fable.

Breaking in between,

their eyes locked with mine,

my heart missed a beat,

for are they real, or just shadows,

drifting through my mind?

They walked towards me,

all at once,

I was speechless,

perplexed by the thought,

"What would they say?",

"How will I respond?".

Amid this rumination,

they passed through me,

vanishing in my heart,

for I fell on the floor,

tears running down my face,

carving silent paths.

I glanced around once more,

no one in sight,

just me and the echoes,

trapped in the gravity of memory's embrace.

6. Cosmic Whispers

"The quiet conversations between the cosmos and the soul—of dreams, destiny, and the eternal question of existence."

A Being in the Infinity

Oh! to be under the stars,

to be surrounded by them,

staring lifelessly into the void,

where a noiseless cry got its stem.

The silence is deafening,

the beauty unparalleled,

Oh! To be a being witnessing this,

like a hug for those never held.

The heart slows its mechanism,

pausing in every beat,

For the vastness, though, surely scary,

quite well contradicts our surfaceness on repeat.

The mind stops racing,

with peace in its vicinity,

Oh! to be under the stars,

to be surrounded by them,

a being in the infinity.

Night sky

I looked up at the night sky,

as I stared at its existence,

when my face was struck softly by a cool breeze,

alleviating the ongoing contemplation in distance.

I am headed towards a journey I'm not sure about,

or maybe I'm not sure if I'm headed towards one,

for there are times I feel,

I've got this,

just a bit of hope and effort mixed in a heavenly ratio,

but isn't rethinking that just a thought away.

I feel like the alleys of an abandoned city,

waiting to be discovered,

having a treasure trove of stories to tell,

but ironically, none to listen to the verse.

I looked up at the night sky,

as I smiled,

with a constant question,

lingering in the corridors of my mind,

Will I turn out to be something,

or is my existence just meant to be turned to dust.

A Life I Might Never Disown

I watch the night sky,

having fascinations of my own,

dreaming of having a life,

I might never disown.

I feel I'm not extraordinary,

to achieve the feats they talk about,

being so normal,

That to be an epitome is just what a voice from somewhere

shouts.

I'm afraid I might end up,

Withering away into nothingness,

Just having things in my head,

so cowardly hiding in distress.

I know it's too much of 'I',

lesser of the larger objective,

But I'm tired, you know,

Ahh here I go again, sorry for being dramatic.

I often look at the night sky,

trying to find some meaning,

But all I have is,

Fascinations of my own,

dreaming of having a life,

I might never disown.

Whispers at Dusk

I stood quietly,

this time not on the run,

silently acknowledging the chaos within,

as my eyes caught hold of the settling sun.

The sky was on the verge of going dark,

unraveling the mysteries hidden,

a pacifying effect on the soul,

when nothing feels forbidden.

"In a universe so big and our time so limited,

Love is all we've got",

How beautiful of someone to think this,

like a warm hug when things feel a lot.

There's an unexplainable feeling nowadays,

slowly boiling up to the surface,

that even the quiet moments in the apricity,

end up making me nervous.

The sun has finally set,

with darkness engulfing the sky,

as I took a deep breath,

looking up, maybe for a reply?

The One With The Moon

You've got scars,

a poignant reminder of what it took to bring you here,

Yet you shine so brightly,

as if you don't care.

But you reveal your only one side,

the one this world's familiar with,

your other facing the emptiness of infinity,

the hidden darker one no less than a myth.

You're an epitome of hope,

the mortals hold on to when darkness prevails,

for a mere reflection of yours,

lifts a sadness, that otherwise entails.

Poets adore you,

your beauty in their musings,

still you hide sometimes,

is it to tend to your bruises?

I know you're looking at me,

Smiling,

pondering on the audacity I have,

to converse with you,

yet my thoughts drift to her, as they always do.

I sighed,

pretending to look elsewhere,

for don't I always do this,
whenever I'm caught vulnerable here and there?

The Final Verse

"Sometimes amidst the chaos,
during moments of uncertainty,
during moments of insecurities,
to get that much needed glimmer of hope,
to pull me back from the dark,
from the steepest of slope,
to know that people can be saved,
to know not to bleed on those who didn't cut you,
for sometimes it's okay to let them be your aid.
To know, among the ups and downs the life offers,
beauty lies in the neutrality,
To know that sometimes things might not go according to you,
but, then, isn't this only reality?
And sometimes during this chaos,
I get my question answered quite right,
as I accept with a smile,
for, that's why I write."

It's been four years since that timid soul, afraid and unaware of the world, first put his tangled thoughts into words. And now, here I am, trembling as I pen the closing note of this book.

Thank you for taking this journey with me, for letting my musings seep into your thoughts. If even a single line of a poem touched your heart, my work here is complete.

www.ingramcontent.com/pod-product-compliance
Lightning Source LLC
Chambersburg PA
CBHW022057150726
47990CB00003B/1130